Criteria of the
Internal Regulations of the
Democratic Parliament

Criteria of the Internal Regulations of the Democratic Parliament

Rasheed EL-MEDAWAR

Professor of constitutional law
at the Hassan II University – Casablanca, Morocco

EL-MEDAWAR, Rasheed, 1964- ...

Criteria of the Internal Regulations of the Democratic Parliament / Rasheed EL-MEDAWAR. – Casablanca: 2020.

40 p. 13,97 X 21,59 cm.

Parliamentary law collection: N°1

includes index

Includes bibliography (p. 28-29)

ISBN: 978-9920-39-621-9

1. The Constitutional law. 2. Parliament. 3. Democracy. 4. the Internal Regulations of the Parliament. 5. Good governance. 6. Political Science (General).

Edition: 1st
CASABLANCA -MOROCOO 2020
Legal Deposit (BNRM): 2020MO1813

CONTENTS

This is a revised and corrected version of the English translation of this study (originally written in Arabic) and published in **"SHURUFAT AL MAJLIS"**, which is a periodical on parliamentary affairs, issued by the State Council in the Sultanate of Oman, in the first issue, April 2016, pages 37-52.

INTRODUCTION

The Internal Regulations of parliaments gain significant importance as they represent the direct distinguished source and the most rich and outstanding among the sources of parliamentary laws[1].

The importance of the Internal Regulations emanates from the importance of the institution whose work they regulate, as they are the most outstanding indicators manifesting the democracy of the political systems. Any parliament cannot carry out its functions effectively, whether at the legislative or oversight of the performance, policies and organs of the executive authority levels, unless its internal regulations regulate its work effectively and efficiently.

In order for the internal regulations of parliaments to be effective and democratic, a number of basic standards must be observed when preparing, drafting or amending them. Respect for these standards will achieve the effectiveness of these regulations in the success, organization and development of democratic parliamentary action. This is what this study seeks to reach through research, analysis and suggestion of these criteria.

---

1 Droit Parlementaire. Pierre Avril / Jean Gicquel, 4eme Edition Montchrestien, 2010, p2.

This paper is seeking to present a scientific definition to the internal regulations of parliaments, and show the importance and necessity of drafting them.

Accordingly, we are discussing the same through three gradual and integrated focal points:

The first focal point: what are the internal regulations?

The second focal point: the importance and necessity of setting the internal regulations;

The third focal point: the standards of the of international regulations for a new parliament.

[I]

WHAT ARE THE INTERNAL REGULATIONS?

At the outset, we have to confess that it is difficult to give a comprehensive definition of the internal regulations of a parliament as reliance on the formal criterion which determines the form and the party which has issued them, as well as the measures adopted in their promulgation of amendment, will not enable us to determine precisely the special nature of the internal regulations of the parliament.

Furthermore, using the formal criterion approach the internal regulations of the parliament to the measures of internal nature. At the same time, that makes them intersect with requirements of constitutional nature, some regulatory and others ordinary, despite the fact that they cannot be of constitutional or legislative or regulatory nature.

To this effect, and to avoid opposition which may arise with regard to the formal criterion, the jurisprudence and the constitutional judiciary have opted to be confined with the objective criterion for the definition of the internal regulations of the parliament.

However, for the purpose of approach to this problem, we would rather merge between the formal and objective criteria.

We shall begin by presenting some close definitions, then try to reach a proposed definition, as per the formal and objective criteria, hoping that it will serve our purpose.

1- Jurisprudence definition of the internal regulations of the parliament

Some legal dictionaries have various definitions for the internal regulations of deliberative parliaments. One constitutional dictionary defines them as: *the decision on which the Assembly votes and contains a group of provisions regulating its work, formation of its organs and functions, and consists of measures that have an appointment of internal organs of the representative assembly, management of deliberations, speech timing, setting measures to be followed for good organization of the discussions and voting for instance, as well as provisions related to other general authorities.*[2]

Another dictionary defined the internal regulations as: a decision determining the methods, and rules of the internal work which should be respected as regards the progress of a council,[3] or as expressed by the Constitutional Dictionary : a preliminary decision taken by the parliament itself on the sidelines of the constitutional requirements which completes the

---

2 Constitutional Dictionary, Judge Mansoor, university corp. for Publication and Distribution, Beirut, 19996, p 1191.

3 Juristic Vocabulary, Gerard Cornu, Puf. Quadrige, Dicos Poche, 8th edition, Paris, 2007, p 790.

parliamentary law[4].

According to Pierre Avril and Jean GICQUEL, the internal regulations of a parliament as per the formal criterion are: a recommendation taken and endorsed by the concerned council as per the regular procedures [depositing a decision, discussing and then endorsing the same in a public setting].

The two jurists have noticed that the administrative law refers internal measures to the rules that have specific competence in its internal topic.

As for the objective criterion, the internal regulations of a parliamentary council represent specificity as regards other written legal rules of the parliamentary law. Paul BASTID says the internal regulations are: the internal law of the same council which has set it. When the council sets its internal regulations , it does not behave as a branch of the legislative authority but as an independent institution which has organizational and disciplinary authority over its members[5], which made Pierre Avril and Jean GICQUEL define the internal regulations by its subject and said: the subject of the parliamentary internal regulations is precisely determined in the organization of the internal work of the council, the procedures adopted for its deliberations, and discipline of its members [6].

---

4 Dictionary of international Law, Thierry Debard, ELLipses Marketing, 2002, p275.

5 Political Institute of the French Parliamentary Monarchy, Paul BASTID, Sirey, 1954, p 260.

6 Parliamentary Law, Pierre AVRIL, Jean GIQUEL, p7 and 8.

According to what has been concluded and decided by Pierre Avril and Jean GICQUEL in their book *The Parliamentary Law* and their approach, Sophie de CACQUERAY said in its university thesis: *the internal regulations of the parliamentary councils, as per the formal criterion, consists of recommendations endorsed by each council and not subject for issuance.* Then she commented on the same and said: using the formal criterion does not enable to precisely determine their nature. In fact, the nature of internal regulations of a parliamentary council cannot be compared to a constitutional or legislative or organic nature. She concluded by saying: it is impossible to reach a formal definition of internal regulations of a parliamentary councils as these internal regulations cannot be balanced or compared to the constitutional or organic or ordinary laws because they are not endorsed by the same procedures, and further its name prevents its comparison with administrative regulations[7]. The internal regulations of a parliament concern a type of an internal law of the council which regulates its work and discipline. It has a special internal legality in parliamentary councils[8].

In an effort to define the internal regulations of parliamentary councils by merging the formal and objective criteria, Yves GUCHET said: *the internal regulations of the parliamentary councils consist of the requirements endorsed by them, related to the mode of its internal organization, work and discipline*[9].

---

7 The Constitutional Council and the Regulations of the Assembly, Sophie de Cacquerray, Economica, , 2001p 324.

8 International Law and Political Institutions, Jean GICQUEL, 24th edition, Paris, Montrestien,2010, p 678 & 679.

9. Parliamentary Law, Yves GUCHET, Economica, Paris, 1996, p 7.

Ali ALSAWI defines the internal regulations of the parliament as: a group of rules related to the work structure of the council, and its main organs. They point out the rights and duties of members, plan, and practice of the various parliamentary functions.[10]

2- Definition of the constitutional judiciary of the internal regulations of the parliament

Other than the jurisprudence, the constitutional judiciary is satisfied with the objective criterion as regards its definition and has not relied on the formal objective.

To this effect, we shall be satisfied with presenting the definition of the constitutional judiciary of the internal regulations in France and Morocco:

The French Constitutional Council has defined the internal regulation of the parliamentary council in two successive decisions, one related to the National Assembly, and the other concerns the Senate, as: *a group of measures and resolutions of internal nature related to the work and internal order of the Council.*[11]

The National Assembly defines its internal regulations as the system which sets all the rules to regulate the work of the Assembly, progress of the legislative procedures, practice of the parliamentary oversight. Any amendment to the regulations shall be

---

10 Development of the Arab Parliamentary Councils, Ali Al Sawi, Plan for Development of the Work of the Arab parliament, Beirut, May 2000, Lebsnese Centre for Studies, First edition, Beirut, 2001, p 295.
11 Decision No.59-2, 24 DC of June 1959 [Regulations of the National Assembly] and decision No. 59-3 DC of 25 June 1959 [Regulations of the Senate].

referred to the Constitutional Council before enforcing the same.[12]

It's worth mentioning that the French practice called the document, as will be pointed out later, the "Regulations" without adding the adjective "Internal" to demonstrate the special nature of this regulatory text without minimizing its legal value and its obligatory power.

The Moroccan constitutional judiciary has been provided with the chance to define the internal regulations of the parliament twice: the *first* at the stage of the constitutional chamber of the Supreme Council, and the *second* at the stage of the constitutional council, as follows:

In the first two resolutions the constitutional chamber has defined the internal regulations of the parliament as " *a group of internal requirements relating to conducting the work of the council and aims at binding the members only*[13], and in another two resolutions it has been expressed that *the internal regulations of the parliament are exigencies falling within the framework of the internal organization and conducting of the work of the council*[14].

The constitutional council has mentioned in the resolution number 405 the issue of internal regulations

---

12 Small Parliamentary Lexical, 2013, in www.assemlee-nationale.fr.

13 Constitutional Chamber, Decisions 1 & 2, 31 Dec. 1963, concerning the Internal Law of the House of Representatives and the Council of Councilors, issued in the official gazette 2672, Jan. 1964, p 50 & 53.

14 Constitutional Chamber decisions 17 & 65concerning the Internal Law of the House of Representatives issued on 19 July 1979 and 21 June 1982 issued in the official gazette No. 3642, 18 Aug, 1982, p 1045.

as *"organization of the internal work of the parliamentary institution and the mode of deliberation*[15] and in the resolution number 829 stated that *the internal regulations of the parliamentary council include requirements aiming at determining the modes and principles which enable the council to regulate its work and carry out its competences as authorized by the constitution*[16].

3- The Proposed Definition

It is remarkable that all the above-mentioned definitions are not general and are not applicable to internal regulations of the parliamentary councils, as they have not taken into consideration the difference in the constitutional and political framework of the governing systems. The internal regulations, as *Ali AL SAWI* says, *are the extension of the constitutional framework and the governing rules of the work of the entire political system. It is therefore the mirror of the political balances and the constitutional intellect in which they have been prepared. They are the gist of the interaction between the requirements of development and the necessities of stability in the work of the parliament.*[17]

The above definitions pertain to the European countries and some Arab states who have adopted their approach.

Other systems of governance have organized the internal affairs of their parliamentary councils by

---

15 Constitutional Council, decision No. 405/2000, 28 June 200, official gazette 4615, 17 July 2000, p 2038.

16 Constitutional Council, decision No. 829/2012, 4 Feb. 2012, official gazette 6021, 13 Feb. 2012, p 655.

17 Draft New Regulations of the Peoples Council, Ali AL Sawi, Al Nahdha Al Arabiyah, Cairo, 2001, p 7.

internal regulations as ordinary laws initiated and endorsed by the parliamentary council itself, as per the legislative procedures, including its issuance and signature by the Head of the state and publication in the Official Bulletin.

For instance, Article 67 of the Yemeni constitution stipulates that the House of Representatives shall set its internal regulations including conduct of the work of the council and its committees and the practice of all its constitutional competences, and the regulations shall not comprise provisions contravening the provisions of the constitution or amending them, and the regulations shall be issued and amended by law[18].

The Jordanian constitution (2011) has stipulated in its Article 83 that each of the two councils draft internal regulations to control and organize its measures and to be presented to the King for endorsement. Article 1 of the internal regulations of the House of Representatives stipulates that it shall be effective as from the date of its publication in the Official Bulletin[19].

Some states have opted for setting the internal regulations by the councils themselves. However, they shall be issued by decrees following the approval of the executive authority. For instance, article 85 of the constitution of UAE stipulates that the National Federal Council shall assume setting its internal regulations which determine its competences and these

---

18 Constitution of the Yemen Republic, issued in 1991 and amended on 29 Feb. 2001.
19 Internal Regulations of the Jordanian House of Representatives 2013, issued on 20 Oct. 2013, published in official gazette 5247.

regulations shall be issued by a decision of the Head of the union as per the approval of the Supreme Federal Council[20].

Some states put as a condition that the internal regulations shall be constitutional before coming into force. The outstanding example is France which has been followed **suit** by some Arab Maghreb States: Morocco, Algeria, Tunisia, and Mauritania. Whereas some regulations made the oversight optional and remote. These are generally the states which have selected the constitutional – judiciary oversight system.

Some regimes have selected the bicameral system while others have selected the unicameral system.

Some of these regimes made these internal regulations of these councils to be issued by a decision which the parliaments take with absolute sovereignty and complete independence from the executive authority. In some applications the internal regulations are initiated by the decision of the executive authority.

Based on that, the status of the internal regulations of the parliament and its legal value vary according to the political system and its constitutional framework. To this effect, each proposed definition of the internal regulations of parliamentary council shall be set as per the constitutional framework of the concerned regime. In application of this criterion the definition we propose for the internal regulations of the parliamentary council conforms with the presidential regimes within the framework of the solid constitutions which are based on special concept

---

20 Constitution of UAE as per amendments of Dec. 2008.

regarding the separation of powers and stipulating their balance and cooperation and endorsing the bicameral system. The internal regulations of each of the two parliamentary councils should be set and should be subject to constitutional oversight before coming into force.

Accordingly, we propose the following definition:

The internal regulations of the parliamentary councils are a group of written legislative requirements, having a special nature, to be set and endorsed by each parliamentary council as per the normal procedures without being subject to the process of issuance, and aims at arranging the special aspects related to the mode of organizing these councils, conducting their work and control of their members. However, they shall not come into force unless being in conformity with the provisions of the constitution.[21]

By analyzing the words of this definition, we conclude the following;

"They are a group of legislative requirements", that means they are not recommendations which confirms its obligatory dimension. They are therefore a set group of legal rules that has all the characteristics of the legal rule: generalization, comprehensiveness, abstraction and commitment.

and "written" free from the unwritten parliamentary concepts and traditions.

---

21 The Issue of the Internal Regulations of the Parliament in the Constitution, Rasheed El-Medawar, collection: "textbooks and academic work", Vol. 111. (REMALD, Ed.) 1 ed., Rabat, Morocco. p 61.

"having special nature" so as to be distinguished from other written legal rules of the parliamentary law, and what is meant is the constitutional, organic and ordinary laws, despite the similarities and intersection among them, whether at the procedures of their endorsement or subject.

This special nature is a point of difference on the level of the internal regulations of the parliamentary councils and their legal value. That led to the difference and discrepancy in their title. In the French application, the legislator opted in Article 61 of the constitution[22] for calling them **"the regulations"** only without adding the term "internal" which makes them like the internal regulations of the local communities and the similar institutions and associations, but he did not call them a law, and they are therefore defined in the French practice as either : the Regulations of the Parliamentary Councils or the Regulations of the National Assembly, or the Regulations of the Senate, or the Regulations of the Parliamentary Conference.

"to be set and endorsed by each parliamentary council" as they should be set and as the competence of setting and voting on them represent an aspect of its independence whether from the executive authority or the other parliament.

As per the ordinary legislative procedures they should be free from the decisions taken by the council through its organs (council bureau presidents' seminar, standing and ad hoc committees and the plenary sessions) outside the framework of the legislative

---

22 The French Constitution of 4 Oct. 1958, date of the constitutional review on 23 July 2008.

procedures. As for the internal regulations of the parliamentary council the procedures necessitate that they should be set in a form of a proposal and forwarded to the concerned council bureau which will in turn refer them to the concerned committee for study and consideration and then submits a report on the same to the plenary session for decision and voting, and shall be considered as endorsed if they gain the relative majority. The term **"ordinary"** is used for distinguishing this procedure from the special procedure concerning the constitutional laws or the organic laws.

And **"without being subject to the process of issuance"** to show that their endorsement procedure lacks the issuance element which as per the legal system hierarchy of the state, if it may be put in order, comes in the fourth place after the constitution, the organic laws and ordinary laws.

"aims at arranging the special aspect" to show that the validity of the internal regulations is limited and does not go beyond the council which has endorsed them and are confined to its internal affairs and should contain requirements related only to the council competences. These are internal requirements concerning the progress of the work of the council and aim at binding the members only. Nothing can be added to them to bind the others without a legislation.[23]

---

23 Constitutional Chamber, decision 1 & 2, 31 Dec. 1963 concerning the two internal Regulations of the House of Representatives and the Council of Councilors of the Moroccan Kingdom, official gazette no. 2672, 10 Jan. 1964, p 50 & 53.

"And shall not come into force unless being in conformity with the provisions of the constitution"; Because the theory of "parliamentary rationalization" (In French: Le parlementarisme rationalisé), as it appeared with the French fifth Republic in 1958 by General Charles de Gaulle and Michel Debre, which aims to prevent the legislative authority from dominating the executive branch, and this philosophy represents the intellectual basis that established the importance and seriousness of the internal regulations of Parliament ; Because setting and interpreting the internal regulations of Parliament, and even not having them, may lead to bypassing the provisions of the constitution; therefore, many constitutions stipulated that internal regulations must be subject to constitutional control before their entry into force. As the subject of the internal regulations of the Parliamentary Councils is considered an extension and a complement to the constitution, which enables parliaments to expand the scope of their oversight, legislative and evaluation terms of reference when it sets its internal regulations by itself or is used by a majority of the numerical government to put an end to the group of rights of parliamentary minorities; therefore, the internal regulations of Parliament must be subject to constitutional oversight By an institution independent of both the legislature and the executive, as a necessity to maintain a balance between them.[24]

––––––––––––––––––––––––––––

24 For reference regarding the Arab experience concerning oversight of the constitutionality of internal regulations of their councils, please refer to our article :" Oversight of the constitutionality of the

Accordingly, the requirements of the internal regulations of the parliamentary council do not complete their legality and take their legal binding value without being in conformity with the provisions of the constitution.

Internal Regulations of constitutional councils in some Arab applications" issued by the Federation of Courts and Constitutional Councils, issue no. 5, Cairo 2014, p 19 to 29.

[II]

THE IMPORTANCE AND NECESSITY OF SETTING THE INTERNAL REGULATIONS

Drafting the internal regulations is regulatory and legislative necessity and a basic tool for the protection of the rights of the political minorities.

1-The internal regulations are a regulatory necessity

The parliamentary councils are a heterogeneous group comprising political factions of discrepant views, different purposes and conflicting interests which will make it difficult to conduct their deliberations and discussions without terms of reference which have the power of the law and should be observed by the members of each council to carry out their work , control the mode of speech and voting and making of decisions, and setting penalties for offenders of these rules and measures. J Rivero says: wherever people meet for deliberations, it is essential that we have a law that regulates these deliberations, and it is practically impossible that such a law shall be dictated on or imposed them from outside. Its argument shall be more powerful if it is initiated and set by the Council itself.[25]

As for the importance of the availability of the internal regulations of the work of the legislative councils, Thomas JEFFERSON , former US President, says in its guide of parliamentary law : the issue is not that the possible laws are the best, the most important thing is to have laws, running the work of the council as per a unified method not subject to the moods of the President or special wishes of each member of the council, and, in conclusion, order , good manners, and harmony should prevail in a council that has high dignity.[26]

Based on the aforementioned, the availability of internal regulations of the parliamentary councils is an indispensable regulatory necessity to guarantee the normal progress of work that regulates these councils.

2- The internal Regulations are a legislative necessity

Someone may say that most of the provisions of the internal regulations are stipulated in the constitution and the various organic laws. The answer is: despite the fact that the constitution and the organic laws have pointed out most of their details, they have been drafted in a general and an overall method and cannot be directly applied in the parliamentary

---

25 Internal Administrative Measures of Order: J. RIVERO, Paris, Sirey, p 177, quoted by S de CACQUERAY in The Constitutional Council and the Regulations of the Assemblies, Thomas JEFFERSON, Stereotype Library, Paris, 1814, p 13.
26 Parliamentary Law Manual, Thomas Jefferson, Stereotype Library, Paris 1814, p8.

councils. This requires a legislative procedure to show and explain what has been outlined in the constitution and the organic laws in a more detailed language determining the timing, modes, and measures for implementing and applying these general requirements. Accordingly, the internal regulations are the applicable provisions for each of the constitution and the organic laws as regards the internal organization of the parliamentary councils.

Do not hesitate therefore to say that setting the internal regulations of the parliamentary councils is a necessity being imposed or a legislative need to fill in the legislative gap emanating from the general and overall constitutional provisions.

3- The internal regulations are a necessity for the protection of minorities

It is well known that the parliamentary councils are based on the majority system, so if there are no rules to arrange and conduct the deliberations and work of the council, the majority will then decide work rules to be observed in making decisions. In this case, the majority will overlook the rules they have set and imposed by their numerical power if applying them will lead to results contradicting their interests in the short run. The big loser in this case is the minority as it is not protected, and the work rules which guarantee their rights are not safeguarded, as it does not possess the immunity against the counter movements of the majority. It is therefore useful for the organization of the internal work of the legislative councils to have unified, written, and stable regulations on which the minority as well as the majority can rely as regards the protection of their rights.

Thomas JEFFERSON, the former US President , says: If the majority in a legislative authority can halt, due to their numerical supremacy, the impact of the non-regular measures they wish to adopt, this minority will then be tyrannized by the majority, if they cannot resort to the rules set for conducting the work and which have gained the nature of the law at the council. The weaker party will therefore be safer through strict observation of these laws and penalizing the offences committed due to the dominant numerical supremacy to curb their contraventions and oppression of any opposition.[27]

Based on the above-mentioned, the availability of internal regulations of a legislative council is a necessity for the protection of the parliamentary minority from the oppression and tyranny of the parliamentary majority.

In conclusion, the setting of internal regulations of parliamentary councils is a regulatory and legislative necessity for the protection of the rights of the political minorities.

---

27 Parliamentary Law Manual, op. cit. p 7 & 8.

[III]

CRITERIA OF THE INTERNAL REGULATIONS FOR A GOOD PARLIAMENT

As has been mentioned in the introduction, in order to have effective internal regulation of the parliamentary legislative council, at least within the margin allowed for them, a number of criteria should be taken into consideration when drafting or amending them. Such criteria will qualify the parliament to carry out its democratic role effectively.

Based on our actual expertise and practice of the parliamentary work, we put forward this endeavor to determine some basic criteria to build internal regulations of a parliamentary democratic parliament.

1- Sovereignty criteria of the parliament on its internal regulations

The first criteria, as we believe, relates to initiation of proposing the internal regulations of the parliament and their amendment. When the parliament sets its regulations by itself, that will oblige the members of the council to commit themselves and follow these regulations. To this effect, J RIVERO says about the internal regulations of the parliamentary council : it's the self-law for conducting their deliberations, and it's the law which will be impossible to dictate or impose on them from outside, and its argument on them should be necessarily more powerful, as it is initiated and set by the council.[28]

It is of paramount importance that the legislative authority should solely draft the procedural rules which control its work and its march, implement and amend the same. This authority, which being used by the legislative organ to control its special procedural rules is actually one of the tools which reflect an indication of its independence and the basic principle of the democratic governance as per the definition of the organization for security and co-operation in Europe (OSCE)[29].

The most important criteria, worthy of attention, at this level are as follows:

I. The parliament shall have full sovereignty and authority to set its internal regulations and competences by taking the initiative of proposing and amending the same, in application of the principle of separation of powers, and in confirmation of the sovereignty of the legislative authority as well as its

---

28 Internal Administrative Measures of Order: J. RIVERO, Paris, Sirey, p 177, quoted by S de CACQUERAY in The Constitutional Council and the Regulations of the Assemblies, Thomas JEFFERSON, Stereotype Library, Paris, 1814, p 13.
29 Development of International Criteria of the Democratic Legislative Authorities, National Democratic Institute for World Affairs [translated by Noor Al Asaad, Beirut, 2007, p 16.

independence from the executive authority in running its internal affairs, as this is considered as an internal affair concerning the parliament. The government and all its executive organs do not need to intervene whether at the level of proposing or reviewing the regulations, or participation in its deliberations. However, the executive authority can reserve the right to challenge the constitutionality of the regulations at the concerned constitutional courts and councils;

II. The scope which the internal regulations organize shall be specified by constitutional provisions or organic laws, and should be stipulated that it should not be violated, and these provisions shall determine the limits separating the scope of law and the scope of the internal regulations of the parliament;

III. The council shall adopt the legislative procedures to which all ordinary law provisions are subject when setting its internal regulations and when amending them. It shall be submitted as a draft at the bureau of the council, to refer it to the concerned committee for consideration. The right of amendment by the members of the concerned council, its discussion in the plenary sitting as per the schedule of the bureau of the council, its endorsement and approval shall be by the majority of the votes. Their issuance shall be subject to the signature of the Chairman only. This means the right of initiation of their proposal and amendment falls within the rights of the members guaranteed by the provisions of the constitution and shall not be restricted by a condition of number or quorum, or timing, and the measures related to their amendment shall be included in the internal regulations themselves.

IV. Without prejudice to the aforementioned right, the internal regulations shall be characterized by stability, sustainability and continuity, as its continued change will disrupt the members whenever new provisions and procedures are introduced.

V. In a bicameral parliamentary system, the members of the two councils shall consult with each other as they represent one parliament and not two separate parliaments. Although each chamber sets its internal regulations and is not committed to what the other sets, it should set the measures for conducting its work in isolation from the other council so that their decisions and measures concerning the procedures and timing shall be consistent and harmonious in such a way that leads to integration and cooperation between the two councils.

2- Criteria guaranteeing the rights of the minorities

Three basic indicators to be endorsed as guarantees for the rights of the minorities:

VI. Setting of mechanisms that guarantee the rights of political opposition, independents, ethnic and linguistic and religious minorities for free expression of their views and thought without being subject to unnecessary pressures, in addition to their relative representation in the internal executive and steering organs of the council.

VII. The partiality, objectivity and integrity of the speakers of parliaments and those of their status, while steering the wok of the council, in application of the right of equality among the members;

VIII. Adopting impartial approaches based on equal opportunities principle, without discrimination in working hours, providing the necessary linguistic facilities for all the members, and in particular the linguistic minority, to be able to conduct their functions in the best possible manner.

3- Transparency criteria in administrative measures

Indicators showing the transparency of the measures of the parliamentary councils:

IX. Ample circulation of information: the Council should have an internal bulletin to be distributed to all the members, a website to post its draft agenda, programs, minutes of deliberations, results of the voting on the legislative provisions, reports on the attendance of the members, as well as justified/unjustified absence from committees meeting and plenary sitting, personal nominations for representation of the council, participation in delegations on external missions, and relevant reports to avail a copy for those who wish that.

X. Setting up internal committees to oversee disbursement of the Council budget: The committee shall comprise all political factions in a relative representation, as the council should not be considered beyond oversight and without prejudice to the right the law accords to the Supreme Council of Accountancy as regards oversight of public finance and ascertain safety of financial transactions related to revenues and expenditures of the parliamentary council and evaluations of the management of its affairs.

4- Criteria of the coherent legislative drafting

The form of the law has a special importance, as there is a controversial relation between the form and the content. A good law is good in form and content.

The good legislative drafting of the internal regulations requires highly technical and professional talents. Whoever is entrusted with drafting them, shall take into consideration a host of important rules as follows:

XI. The criteria of construction, organization, and engineering: at the outset a design should be laid down for the general structure of the text with a view to a coherent and harmonious structure. To this effect, all divisions, chapters and articles should be logically arranged taking into consideration the realistic sequence of the matters and the unity of the topic. To achieve this, the major and sub-titles, as well as the division of paragraph should be set in clear and separate units. Provisions should be presented and divided into numerical forms. Finally, detailed contents should be set as a guide to easily find the required provisions.

XII. Precision and clarity criterion: Whoever draft the regulations should select clear, specific, and precise words, and avoid ambiguous, vague and confounding ones. He should refrain from synonyms, repetition and adjectives as well as redundancy and circumlocution. Further, he should observe the grammar, and use verbal phrases in the present simple tense, and avoid as much as possible using noun phrases.

CONCLUSION

We have tried in this paper to present a vision merging the theory and the application. That is the theorization based on the practice and experience. We have undoubtedly demonstrated the importance of the internal regulations of the parliamentary councils, and that setting them is not only a technical matter, but in addition to that a political work and ,therefore, needs consolidation of the efforts of high specialized qualifications, and at the same time, qualified cadres in the parliamentary work.

Based on the above-mentioned, we recommend:

The necessity of furnishing the parliamentary councils with efficient administration, coupled with human resources possessing high technical expertise in the technology and methods of drafting legislations to be tasked with conducting studies, providing the necessary information related to constitutional, legal, and political updates. All this should be translated into a preliminary draft of the internal regulations of the council. In light of the constitutional and political changes, the administration should put the viability and draft of the internal regulations on the desk of the Chairman upon his election to assume taking the measures to complete the legislative procedures along with the members of the Council. In other words, the administration precedes the events and carries out what is known as the formal legislative process which is assumed by the drafter of the legislative provisions. This shall be followed by the role of the parliamentarians to include the political nature in the text of the internal regulations. This represents the second aspect of the process which is known as the legislative-political process.

It is necessary that a special committee comprising a group of the members of the council tasked with regulatory responsibilities [the Chairman of the council, members of the bureau of the council, heads of the standing committees, heads of the parliamentary teams] should assume consideration and study of the proposals of the internal regulations and their amendments. As per their expertise and responsibilities, they are the most capable to propose amendments, assimilate, understand, and discuss them with other members whose participations are sometimes off-point and hinder positive proposals.

REFERENCES

- <u>**In Arabic:**</u>

Development of International Criteria of the Democratic Legislative Institutions, National Democratic Institute for Int. Aff., Translated by Noor Al Asaad, Beirut, 2007.

Development of the Work of Parliamentary Arab Councils, Papers of the Parliamentary Seminar, Beirut, May 2000, Lebanese Centre for Studies, First edition, Beirut 2001.

Draft New Regulations of the Peoples Council. Ali Al Sawi, Arabian Nahdha House, Cairo, 2001.

Internal Regulations of the Jordanian House of Representatives 2013, issued on 220 October 2013, published in the Official Bulletin n° 5247.

The Constitution of the Jordanian Kingdom, 2011 House of Representatives Publications, Jordan, 2011.

The Constitution of the Kingdom of Morocco, Promulgate by the Dahir n° 1.11.91 from July 29, 2011, RABAT: Official Bulletin, Vol. 5964 BIS, p 3600

The Constitution of the Yemeni Rep., issued in 1991, amended on 20 Feb, 2001.

The Constitution of UAE, as per amendments in 2008, issued by the Sec, Gen. of the National Federal Council 2010.

The Constitutional Dictionary, Olivier Duhamel and Yves Mény, translated by Mansoor AL Qadi, revised by Zuhair Shukr, University Institution for Publication, Studies and Distribution, First Edition, Beirut, 1996.

The Issue of the Internal Regulations of the Parliament in the Constitution, Rasheed El-MEDAWAR, collection: "textbooks and academic work", Vol. 111. (REMALD, Ed.) 1 ed., Rabat, Morocco.

- **In French and English**

Dictionary of International law, Thierry DEBARD, Ellipses Marketing, 2002.

French Constitution of 4 October 1958, constitutional revision of 23 July 2008.

International Law and Political Institutions, Jean GICQUEL et Jean-eric GICQUEL, 24th edition, Paris, Montchrestien, 2010.

Juristic Vocabulary, Gerard Cornu, Puf. Quadrige, Dicos Poche, 8th edition, Paris, 2007.

Parliamentary Law Manual, Thomas JEFFERSON, Stereotype Library, Paris, 1814.

Parliamentary law, Pierre Avril/Jean GICQUEL, 4th edition, Montchrestien 2010.

Parliamentary law, Yves GUCHET, Economia, Paris, 1996.

Small Parliamentary Lexical, 2013 in www, assemblee-natioanle.fr

The Constitutional Council and the Regulations of the Assembly, Sophie de Cacqueray, Economica. Paris, 2001.

The Political Institutions and the French Parliamentary Monarchy, [1814-1848], Payl BASTID, Sirey, 1954.

ABOUT THE AUTHOR

Rashid Al-Medawar

Birth: 1964 in Casablanca- Morocco;

Professor of constitutional law at the Hassan II University – Casablanca, Morocco;

Doctor of Laws, University of Muhammad V, Faculty of Law, Agdal / Rabat;

Doctor of Higher Islamic, University of Al-Karaouine, Dar Al-Hadith Al-Hassania Foundation, Rabat.

Tasks and responsibilities:

He was previously elected as a deputy in the House of Representatives for three consecutive terms (1997-2008), as Vice President of the Moroccan Parliament (2002-2004), and a former member of the Constitutional Council of the Kingdom of Morocco (2008-2017).

He wrote a number of books in Arabic on parliamentary law and constitutional jurisdiction:

1. Parliament in light of the new constitution, Series of Books in Parliamentary Law, No. 1, Rabat 2019;

2. Constitutional judiciary and internal regulations of Parliament 1963-2016, Public Dialogue Series, No. 11, Rabat (2016);

3. The Issue of the Internal Regulations of the Parliament in the Constitution, Rashid El-Medawar, collection: "textbooks and academic work", Vol. 111. (REMALD, Ed.) 1 ed., Rabat, Morocco.

4. controls the Constitutionality of the Internal Regulations of Parliament in Morocco: characteristics and Procedure, Rabat (2008);

5. parliamentary work in Morocco: Issues and Problems, Rabat (2006);

6. Internal Regulations of the House of Representatives: Study and Commentary, Parliamentary Publications, Rabat (2005).

rachidmedouar@gmail.com

https://orcid.org/0000-0002-6614-0343

Completed printing in 2020 in MOROCCO by

DECOLOR PRINTING

BD LAYMOUNE LOT KENZA II N°68 OULFA-CASABLANCA

Legal deposit: May 2020

www.ingramcontent.com/pod-product-compliance
Lightning Source LLC
Chambersburg PA
CBHW061320140726

47998CB00006B/2482